CHIN-NA:
The Grappling Art of
Self-Defense

CHIN-NA:
The Grappling Art of Self-Defense

by Willy Lin

Edited by Bill Griffeth

Graphic Design by Karen Massad

©1981, Ohara Publications, Incorporated
All Rights Reserved
Printed in the United States of America
Library of Congress Catalog Card Number: 81-82586

ISBN-10: 0-89750-076-8
ISBN-13: 978-0-89750-076-0

Fourteenth printing 2007

WARNING

BLACK BELT BOOKS
A Division of **OHARA** **PUBLICATIONS, INC.**
World Leader in Martial Arts Publications

Dedication

This book is dedicated to all those students and instructors of the T'ien Shan P'ai who have carried forward our traditions from the past, and who will continue to share the teachings of the P'ai as a bridge into the future.

Acknowledgements

Without the help of a number of people, this volume could never have been published. I would like to express my sincere appreciation to all whose collective participation has made it possible: my brother, Tony Lin, and my assistants, Christopher Pei, John Norris and Stuart Meyer for their help; Bill Griffeth and his staff at Ohara Publications for their encouragement; Brian Lowe for his photography; and Laurie and David Pearlstein for their patience throughout the whole undertaking. I would like to also give a special thanks to Pat Hurston for unequaled help and support in preparing and editing this text.

About the Author

Willy Lin was born in Tai Chung, Taiwan, in 1938. He studied martial arts intensively from 1959 to 1968 under the guidance of Wang Jyne Jen, who is known as the sole inheritor of the robe and bowl of the T'ien Shan P'ai (or the Celestial Mountain School of Chinese Boxing). Lin eventually became Wang's full-time teaching assistant and disciple.

In 1968, Lin left Taiwan for Sao Paulo, Brazil. There he taught various forms of boxing and other martial arts for the Chinese Association Center in that city. He came to the United States in 1970, and a year later he opened his first school in Silver Spring, Maryland. That one school has grown and developed into several in and around the nation's capital.

Lin has done a great deal to promote an understanding of the martial arts both in the immediate Washington, D.C. area and throughout the country. He has sponsored touring companies offering performances of the various aspects of T'ien Shan P'ai; he has participated in international demonstrations; he has appeared on both local and national television (including ABC's *Wide World of Sports*); and he has participated in major physical fitness programs such as "Healthworks '79" which was sponsored by the U.S. Department of Health, Education and Welfare. Lin has also appeared in educational films made for the U.S. Department of the Navy. Additionally, he has organized programs to introduce senior citizens to the benefits of the exercise of T'ai Chi Ch'uan.

Lin's philosophy supports the concept that the primary function of the martial arts is the perfection of a person's life. Perfection, in this sense, encompasses the preservation of health, remedies for physical and mental weaknesses, and the improvement of personality and temperament. Lin's fondest desire is to familiarize all who are interested with his art of T'ien Shan P'ai. Through his art, he hopes to share his culture and his heritage by making the knowledge of it available to the greater American public.

Introduction

You are leisurely strolling through your local park one fine autumn evening when you are grabbed from behind by some thug demanding money. But the surprise is on him. Before he can even say the word "wallet" you have him by the wrist or the thumb or the elbow, and with the least amount of effort, you literally bring him to his knees.

And so it goes with the *Chin-Na* style of T'ien Shan P'ai kung fu, an ageless form of opponent control that hasn't changed in centuries. Still as simple as the day it was first developed, in the right hands it is among the most effective streetfighting techniques being used today. The practitioner quickly seeks out some natural weakness in the body of his attacker, grasps it and manipulates it effectively.

But while it may look easy, the simplicity is in the lack of effort, not the lack of skill. The skill comes from hours of practice under the tutelage of a knowledgeable instructor or a good instructional text.

Chin-Na: The Grappling Art of Self-Defense is divided into two parts. The first part, Principles, outlines the whole basic theory behind Chin-Na. Chapter one shows good warm-up exercises designed to loosen the parts of your body that will be used in the techniques outlined later in the book. Chapter two illustrates those parts of the body which are most vulnerable to a Chin-Na hold. Chapter three shows you variations of the most basic technique in Chin-Na, the quick release. And chapter four outlines several quick-release techniques for you to practice and master.

Part two, Execution, contains six chapters each dedicated to defenses against a specific hold. They include the hair grab, the neck grab, the chest grab, the upper arm grab, the forearm grab and the wrist grab. These are the more advanced techniques of Chin-Na, and they should only be practiced after the quick-release techniques of chapter four have been mastered.

One last word. Chin-Na is primarily a defensive, rather than an offensive, style. It was developed for opponent control, as a response to an attack. Students should always remember that Chin-Na techniques should never be used to break bones or to bring opponents great harm.

Willy Lin has done a fine job of compiling this book. It provides the reader with a broad idea of the most basic tenets in Chin-Na. If they are practiced regularly and properly, a dedicated student should be able to effectively defend him/herself against attacks from any angle, on any part of the body.

—Ohara Publications

Author's Preface

This is a book about the Chinese art of Chin-Na, the grappling technique used in Chinese boxing. It is designed to serve as a manual for serious students who are interested in mastering the basic principles of this centuries-old form of self-defense.

It is often said that no book can compare to studying under the guidance of a qualified instructor. For the most part, this opinion is valid. However, given the limitations of a book format, I feel this volume is as clear a statement of the art of Chin-Na as is possible to communicate, short of personal supervision. If the reader will be as exacting in his practice as I have tried to be in compiling the text and in detailing the pictures, then he will find the book of real value.

Chin-Na is one of the most sophisticated forms of self-defense to ever come out of China. It employs highly-skilled hand and foot techniques to completely control the movement of an opponent. When done properly, Chin-Na techniques reduce the opponent to a state of immobility and helplessness. The adversary is left terrorized because he is so easily controlled.

In order to become a good Chin-Na practitioner, some basic qualities must be understood, and certain abilities must be developed. The most important qualities required are sure senses of judgement, response, speed and strength. In addition to this general control, the student must be able to evaluate both his opponent and the circumstances that arise from, or are developed during, a given threatening situation.

Having sound judgement determines better than half the success of a Chin-Na artist. Bad judgement not only makes an action ineffective, but it is also the single-most common factor leading to a defeat. You must learn to size up situations *before* they occur, as well as during an actual conflict. By correctly anticipating an opponent's action, or reaction, you can most effectively select which of your many techniques will be most advantageous.

In order to develop a sense of sound judgement, the student must strive to become sensitive to the responses of his opponent. Before you take any definite action, you must pay complete attention to any changes in your opponent's activity. Certain actions are movement for the sake of movement. Such moves are not any real threat. They must be differentiated from those actions which signal the beginning of a true attack. It is critical that you learn to read these two types of movements—the feint and the true attack—quickly and correctly. Once it is determined that an attack is actually starting, the response must be immediate. The accuracy of your judgement is your chief weapon in winning an advantage.

In addition to making accurate judgements, you must train yourself to react with split-second speed. The faster you can move, the greater the chance to control your opponent. While using the art of Chin-Na, if you are a little late with a response it can be disastrous. If the timing is off, you will miss your hold, and you will not be able to apply the technique in the correct manner.

Chin-Na is one of the most convenient of the martial arts to study. It requires no great amount of practice space and no special or protective clothing or devices. But it does require a reliable partner with whom to practice. Training by oneself does not produce any true progress, and, in fact, it only gives the student a sense of false confidence in his ability. To have two or more practice partners is even more advantageous when studying Chin-Na. In this manner, everyone can experience the techniques of controlling and feel what it is like to be controlled. The greater the variety of the partners, the more experience the student will gain and the quicker and more completely the techniques will be mastered.

With the possible exception of T'ai Chi Ch'uan (as taught for its practical, or fighting, applications) I think it is fair to say that Chin-Na utilizes the understanding of psychology more than any other martial art system. In T'ai Chi Ch'uan there is a saying: *Let four ounces of strength repel one thousand pounds.*

In practical application, T'ai Chi develops its tactics according to these words. For example, if a practitioner pretends to hit the upper portion of an opponent's body, the ultimate aim and subsequent strike should be to the lower portion. If he wants to attack the left, he feints to the right until his opponent drops his guard and allows the attack on the left to succeed.

Similar techniques are called upon in Chin-Na. If you want to grasp the right hand of your opponent, pretend to turn it loose. At the point when the opponent uses that same hand for his attack, you are in a position to catch it and use his own momentum against him.

As you will learn, Chin-Na techniques have this emphasis on psychology built in to the movements. The techniques were formulated with both the mental and physical components in balance, and for this reason, the art is very elegant. With the proper use of basic fighting psychology, plus the wide variety of techniques available through the Chin-Na, the practitioner can force his opponent to expose his weak points.

Chin-Na, in my opinion, is one of the best systems of self-defense ever devised. It is particularly effective in close fighting, and for that reason, its techniques are used by law enforcement agencies all over the world.

This book is designed to acquaint you with basic Chin-Na techniques. As you digest the material, you should come to an understanding of the theory behind the technique. The theory is the true key to understanding, rather than just doing the Chin-Na. As you master this understanding, you master the art of Chin-Na, that creative element which allows you the freedom to improvise correctly using the techniques if called upon to do so. No one can teach you how to understand. That sensitivity is only acquired through practice, concentration to detail, and patience. With diligence, you will come to know the underlying patterns of the Chin-Na action. You will come to feel the correctness of the angles of pressure as they are applied to the different parts of the body. Once this knowledge of angles and pressures becomes a part of your body's fighting vocabulary, you will be able to respond fluently to any threatening situation automatically and appropriately.

This manual is designed to share my knowledge with you, the student, through words, through directions and through pictures. It is my hope that your own participation and interest will supply the other half of the dialogue so that you, too, may come to an understanding of this centuries-old art of self-defense.

Willy Lin
Washington, D.C., 1981

Training Tips
Before You Practice

When Chin-Na techniques are used, little real strength is actually needed. If they are executed correctly, the techniques are effortless. And therein lies both the beauty and the danger of the Chin-Na.

Chin-Na works by twisting or applying pressure to certain joints in the body. Using too much strength could easily break an opponent's bone or snap his tendon. Where power is essential in a fighting situation, using too much strength in practice can be dangerous. Because it is difficult for a

beginning student to realize how much pressure he is actually exerting, he must be constantly on guard not to injure his partner during practice.

The first practice principle that a student must master is to remember actions clearly. It is better to learn and practice one single movement precisely than to try to learn too much too fast. The accumulation of precise actions can be productive, whereas the stockpiling of unclear actions is a waste of time.

Next, the student must strive for a high degree of accuracy in remembering the sequence of the movements for each technique. This is particularly important because if the sequence of a technique is confused or reversed, the angles of pressure will be incorrect, and the technique will fail. For this reason, I have numbered the order of movements in each of the techniques as clearly as possible.

Your rate of practice determines your control; speed improves gradually as the student becomes more and more skilled. Therefore, each action should be practiced slowly and with controlled strength. In this way no one will be accidentally hurt. In addition, the student will learn exactly how much strength he needs to apply to a technique in order to be effective.

The actions of a technique must be practiced until they are well coordinated. The student must learn to save his own power and waste no energy applying the technique. A man's power is best used when it flows easily and naturally, rather than as a tense display of strength countering strength.

It cannot be overemphasized that control must be learned. Beginning students must be constantly reminded to control their strength during a training session. A split second of carelessness may result in a broken bone or a strained tendon for the practice partner. Therefore, when two or three persons are training together, mutual understandings and/or signals must be employed. Once these signals are agreed upon, training can proceed.

The practice partner should experience a little discomfort when the technique is applied, or the student will not be certain he has found the proper angle of pressure. However, as soon as the partner gives the prearranged signal, he must be released *at once*.

There are a few additional points I would like to pass on to the student of Chin-Na. I suggest you do some basic warm-up exercises before you undertake any training session. That way, you will not risk straining your body or pulling a muscle.

Secondly, try to cultivate a calm mind, a good temperament, and patience so that you can react with appropriate authority in a threatening situation. It goes without saying that you should never practice Chin-Na when you are not in complete control of yourself. Specifically, drugs and alcohol do not mix with this art. It would be highly irresponsible to consider practicing while under their influence.

Similarly, do not practice Chin-Na against a partner who is much weaker than yourself. To practice with such a person would only lead to problems, because your individual senses of strength would be so different. If your practice partner has a physical handicap where he is unable to hear or speak, be extra careful to work out a non-verbal signal which means "release the hold."

Remember, in order to learn to do Chin-Na properly, you should execute the technique until your opponent feels some pain. At the same time, you must remain in complete control of how much pressure you are applying so that accidents will not happen. If you take care, are patient, and practice in an exacting manner, you should be successful in your personal training of the Chin-Na.

Contents

PART I
Principles

Chapter I

BASIC PREPARATIONS

This chapter demonstrates the ten basic warm-up exercises which should all be performed before any Chin-Na training is undertaken. They serve to limber each group of muscles in the body in order to reduce the risk of injury by pulling or tearing muscles which are too "cold" to work.

Special attention should be given to the stances. These positions form the foundation of good balance which is necessary for the successful practice of Chin-Na.

MA BU STANCE

To assume the ma bu position, spread your feet out about twice the width of your shoulders, bending your knees forward slightly. Distribute your weight equally—50 percent of it on each foot—and keep your feet parallel to each other. Hold your body erect, but let your buttocks protrude backward. This should bring your knees and feet into alignment so that straight lines

FRONT VIEW

KUNG BU STANCE

To enter the kung bu position, as you shift 60 percent of your weight to your forward leg, bend your forward knee 90 degrees. At the same time, extend your rear leg straight behind you, with your knee locked, distributing the balance of your weight to it. Turn your forward foot inward 45 degrees to afford fast, effective protection for your groin area.

FRONT VIEW

may be drawn from your head through your left knee and foot and through your right knee and foot. The ma bu position is particularly powerful against side attacks, and continuous practice builds strong leg muscles. Ideally, the student should be able to hold a ma bu stance for 30 uninterrupted minutes.

SIDE VIEW

Turn your rear foot outward 45 degrees so that both feet are parallel to each other. Make sure that your forward knee lies directly in front of your forward hip and that your forward foot is directly under your forward knee. The kung bu stance is especially effective against frontal attacks.

SIDE VIEW

EXERCISE I
Part One

Start (1) in a relaxed position with your feet together. Then (2&3) raise your arms, with your palms facing up, until your hands touch over your head. With your palms still touching (4) pull your hands straight down in front of your chest and stop (5) when your hands reach chest level. Interlock (6) the fingers of both hands and (7) rotate your clasped hands inward toward your body. Then (8) push upward until your arms are fully extended, with your palms facing toward the ceiling. Finally (9-11) lower your hands slowly back down to your sides. Repeat this exercise two more times.

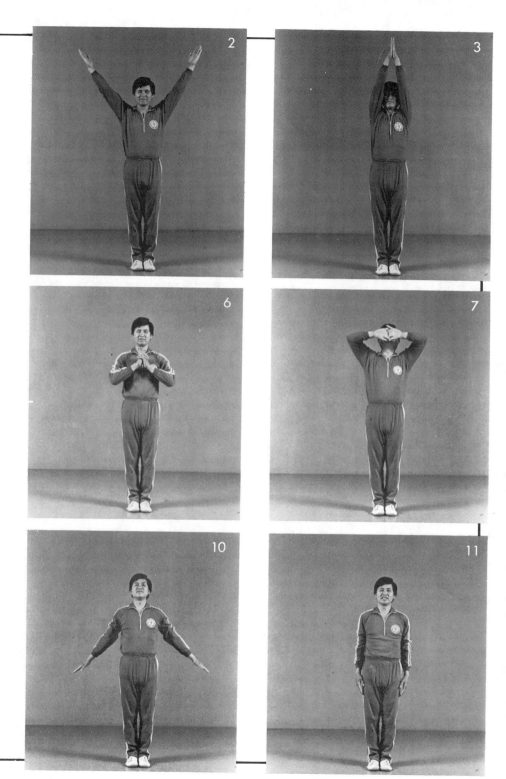

EXERCISE I
Part Two

Begin (1) in the fully extended vertical position with your palms facing toward the ceiling. Then (2-9) twist your body to the right in a circular clockwise direction until you return to the fully extended vertical position. (Note that you should lean forward slightly while completing the circle.) Repeat the movement two more times. Next

Continued on next page

(10-17), repeat the same motion to the left in a counterclockwise direction, and repeat that two more times. With your fingers still locked (18-22) bend over and touch the floor in front of you and return to the standing position. Then (23-27) repeat that motion to the right and (28-32) to the left. Finally

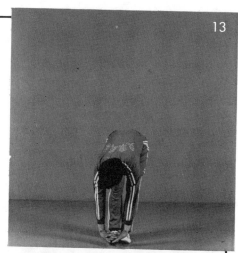

Continued on next page

Continued from preceding page

(33-38) bend forward and touch the floor, then rise to a standing position and continue to raise your arms through the fully extended vertical

21

24

25

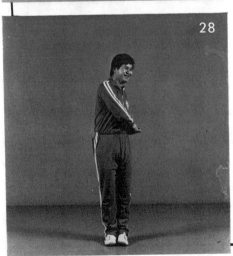

28

29

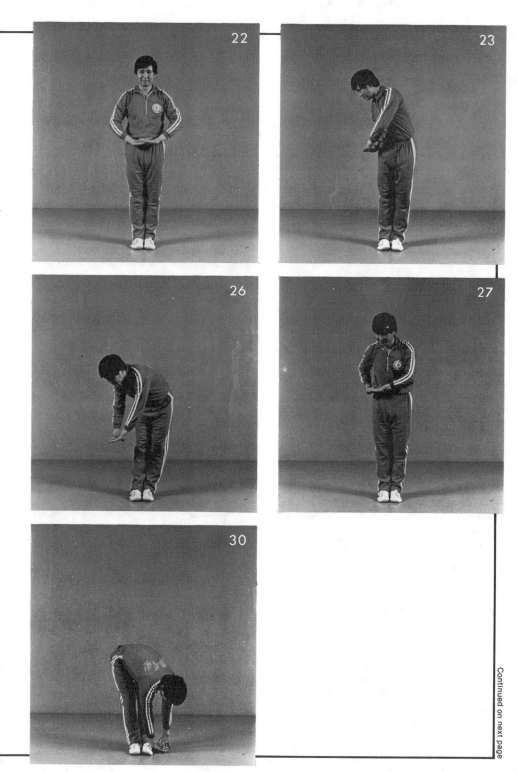

Continued on next page

position. Unclasp your hands (39) and lower them to your side with your palms down and finish (40) in a relaxed position.

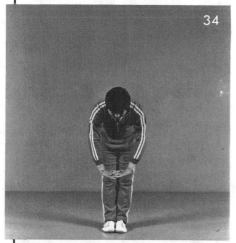

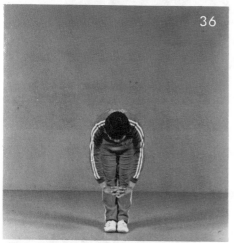

EXERCISE II

Begin (1) by standing erect with your feet slightly apart and your left fist clenched. With an upward sweep (2) bring your right hand in front of you in a circular counterclockwise motion. Continue this movement (3-5) swinging

Continued on next page

7

your arm out to the right side.
Straighten your elbow as you go. As
your right arm comes down to a position in front of your midsection (6-11)
begin an upward sweep with your left
hand, swinging it out to the left side in
front of you in a circular counterclockwise motion. When your right arm

10

Continued on next page

13

**CRANE BEAK WRIST
(DETAIL)**

has completed 1½ rotations (12) stop
it in front of your chest and hook your
left hand into a crane beak. Then (13)
move your right leg forward into a
45-degree angle, placing your weight
on your left leg. Bend forward (14-16)
and touch the toes of your right foot
(17) with your right elbow.

15

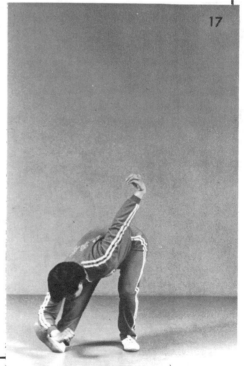

EXERCISE III

Begin (1) in the ma bu stance with your hands on your knees. Then (2) slowly bend your right knee, going down as far as possible. Straighten your left leg and lock it. Keep both feet stationary and flat on the floor throughout the exercise. (As a variation, especially for the beginner, keep only the heel of your outstretched foot on the floor.) Passing through the ma bu stance (3) bend your left knee, going down as far as possible. Again, keep both feet stationary and flat on the floor. Straighten your right knee (4) and lock it as you lower yourself to the floor. Alternate the knee bends until you have done a total of ten times on each side.

EXERCISE IV

From a kung bu stance with your left foot forward (1) step back as far as possible with the toes of your right foot. Hold your hands on your hips. Bend down (2) on your left knee until your slightly bent right knee almost touches the floor. Remember to keep your feet stationary. Repeat this bending movement 20 times.

43

EXERCISE V

Begin (1) in an upright position with your feet spread about two shoulder-widths apart, and place your hands on your hips. Remember to keep your knees locked throughout the exercise. Bend at the waist (2&3) leaning to the right and slide your right hand down the outside of your right leg to touch your foot. Keep your left hand on your left hip. Sweep your right hand (4-7) to your left foot in a wide, circular movement across the floor. Then (8-12) bring it back to its point of origin on your

Continued on next page

right hip. Twist your torso to accommodate the sweep of your hand. Then (13&14) with both hands on your hips, touch the floor in front of you with your head three times and (15) return to an upright position. Bend (16) at the waist. Again (17-19) slide your right hand down the outside of your right leg and sweep it across the floor in a wide circle. However, instead of touching your left foot, grab the outside of your left ankle. Finally (20) touch your left knee with your head three times.

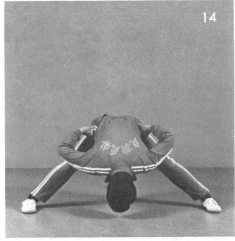

EXERCISE VI

Place your hands on your knees (1) keeping your feet together and your knees bent. Move your knees (2) in a counterclockwise circle to the left, then (3) clockwise to the right. Straighten up (4) and stand erect with your hands on your hips. Next (5-8) loosen the toes and ankle of your right foot by circling it on the floor to your side. Do the same with your left foot. At the same time, hold your arms out slightly and shake your fingers.

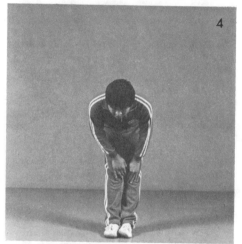

EXERCISE VII

Assume a left foot forward kung bu stance (1) with your left hand on your left hip, your right arm at your side, your elbow straight and your fist clenched. Swing your right fist forward (2-5) up and backward in a relaxed circular motion. Assume an upright, standing position (6) with your legs straight, your feet about one shoulder-width apart and your arms raised. Repeat (7-11) the circling of your arms, moving them simultaneously in opposite directions, and swing your left arm forward and your right arm back. Then (12-15) circle both arms upward

Continued on next page

and backward three times, crossing
them in front of you each time. At the
end of the third swing (16) bend backwards at the waist and extend your
arms. Let your head drop back also,
and hold this position for a few seconds. Resume your upright position
(17-19) as you circle both your arms
downward and back three times, again
crossing them in front of you. At the
end of the third swing (20&21) bend forward at the waist with your head down,
and your arms extended up toward the
ceiling. Hold this position for a few
seconds.

EXERCISE VIII

Begin (1) in a standing position, with your feet spread about two shoulder-widths apart, your body turned to the right, and both arms extended out to that side. Using your waist as a pivot, outline a 360-degree clockwise sweep with your extended hands, (2) drop them down to the floor, (3) bring them up to your left and (4-7) raise them high

Continued on next page

Continued from preceding page

above your head, leaning backward as you do so. Continue the circle (8-11) and after you have completed 1½ rotations and are facing to your left (12) extend your right arm out to the left and (13&14) follow that with your left. Perform this sequence, both clockwise and counterclockwise, five times each.

EXERCISE IX

With your hands on your hips and your feet spread about shoulder-width (1&2) bend backwards as far as possible. Then (3&4) swing your arms behind you and bring them forward. As you do that (5&6) bend over and touch the floor, keeping your knees straight.

EXERCISE X

Assume a ma bu stance (1) with your arms crossed in front of you resting on your knees. Then (2-7) roll your head down and around in a clockwise rotation. Next (8) turn your head to the left, then (9) to the right and finally (10) face front again.

61

Chapter II

PRESSURE POINTS

In order to understand Chin-Na and why it works the way it does, it is necessary to have a concept of the Oriental scheme of *pressure points*. A pressure, or vital, point is a location on the body which, when touched, squeezed, struck or compressed in some way, causes internal reactions.

The ancient Chinese first understood, and even diagrammed these locations thousands of years ago. However, because of the potentially lethal aspects of the vital point, this knowledge remained a great secret available to only the most trusted disciples. Even today, very few reliable texts have appeared in print on this delicate subject.

Physiologically, a pressure point is an aspect of the nervous system. Depending on which point is touched, and the manner in which it is touched, the reaction to the pressure can be immediate or delayed. And the effect can be twofold: it may cause damage to the internal organ itself, and/or it may simply send waves of pain to the brain.

T'ien Shan P'ai's Chin-Na is so highly refined that it utilizes only about

14 pressure points in order to achieve its desired effects. (Six of these locations are pictured on pages 64-65.) Notice that most of the points are located on the limbs, that they are different from the more commonly diagrammed acupuncture points, and that they do not relate to the vital, or lethal, cavities (spaces) most of which are found along the central portion of the body.

Ideally, the Chin-Na artist should not have to touch any actual pressure point with his own hand in order to gain the desired advantage. Instead, he need only apply general pressure to the opponent's nervous system by manipulating his adversary's bones and tendons. The result is that the opponent becomes his own worst enemy, because the more he struggles to overcome the Chin-Na, the more pressure his own body places against its nervous system.

T'ien Shan P'ai's system of Chin-Na is not really concerned with the lethal vital points. The reason for this is that its goal is merely to control an opponent efficiently, with style and with a natural flow of energy. The point is not to maim or kill.

Similarly, there is no reason why injuries should occur during the practice of Chin-Na. Accidental injuries happen only when there is not sufficient control maintained. T'ien Shan P'ai does not advocate anticipating injuries, because that only causes anxiety in the student and his partner, and it gets in the way of maintaining the clear mind necessary for constructive practice. Partners must be able to trust each other enough to allow themselves to experience the techniques without worrying about injury. Otherwise, the spirit of the art is lost in sadistic manipulations.

The nervous system of the human body is the network of all motor and mental processes. It is probably the body's most delicate and critical system. For this reason, the pressure points (the openings or gateways to that system) must be treated with respect.

The potential for doing serious harm to a joint or bone is always present when applying any Chin-Na. The student will become more and more aware of this truth as his practice progresses. It is for this reason that T'ien Shan P'ai stresses control, especially in the early stages of training. The point is not to cause students to become irresponsibly "drunk" on the power the techniques provide them with.

Applying Chin-Na against the vital or lethal cavaties of the body changes the psychological intention of the technique. Chin-Na is most effective as a *reaction* to an assault. While it is true that you can attack with Chin-Na, T'ien Shan P'ai has other *chuans* (fists), such as Shao-Lin, Pa-Kua, Hsing-i or Tai-Chi, which are infinitely more efficient and appropriate if a life-threatening situation demands more aggressive action.

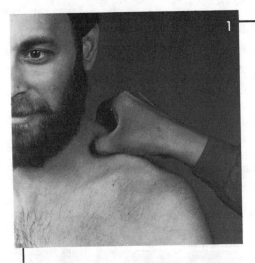

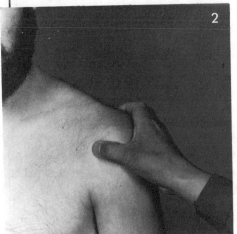

PRESSURE POINTS

The six most basic pressure points on the body used in Chin-Na are located on the upper part of the body since they are the most readily accessible.

They are (1) the base of the neck, (2)

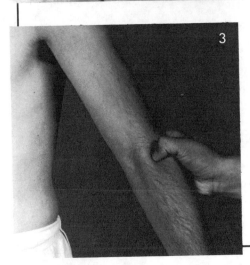

the point of the shoulder, (3) the outside of the elbow, (4) the inside of the
elbow and (5) the section on the hand
between the base of the thumb and
the index finger.

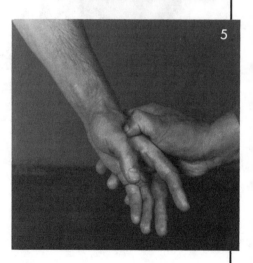

Chapter III

THE QUICK RELEASE

The most basic techniques of T'ien Shan P'ai's Chin-Na relate to the *quick release*. These defenses require that pressure be applied against the attacker's thumb. The releases are intended to be extremely fast techniques, and they must be practiced until they are the conditioned responses to a given grab. The defender's reaction must become automatic, appropriate, and immediate; in short, a reflex action. Each release can be done with either hand, and the student must practice them with both hands for any eventuality.

The following four sequences of pictures show the details of what happens when pressure is applied against the thumb in the four basic positions. Learn the principle demonstrated in each of them carefully. This principle will occur again and again throughout this section as the final movement necessary to break any hold in the quick release.

PARTS OF THE HAND

Before quick releases can be practiced, it is necessary to introduce some basic vocabulary for the parts of the hand as it is used in Chin-Na. Familiarize yourself with the points indicated in the accompanying photographs. These locations will be of great use in both understanding and applying the Chin-Na techniques correctly.

FRONT OF HAND (PALM)
A. Edge (inside)
B. Heel
C. Wrist Joint
D. Palm Heart

BACK OF HAND
E. Edge (outside)
F. Tiger Mouth
G. Wrist Joint (outside)
H. Center

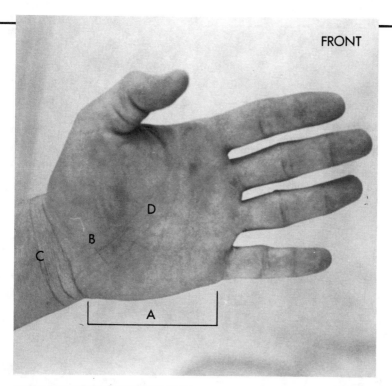

FRONT

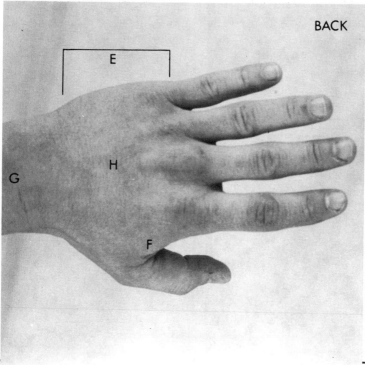

BACK

RIGHT WRIST GRAB (ARM UP)

The attacker grabs (1) the defender's right wrist while both arms are up. The defender (2-4) turns his arm downward in a clockwise direction, applying pressure against the attacker's thumb. The result (5) is that the hold is broken.

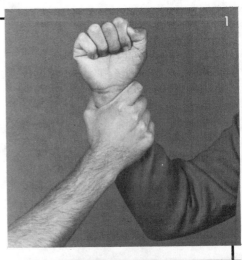

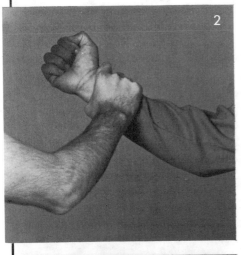

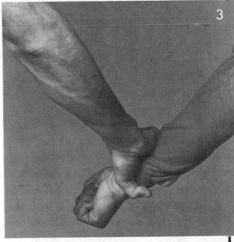

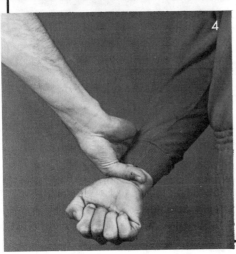

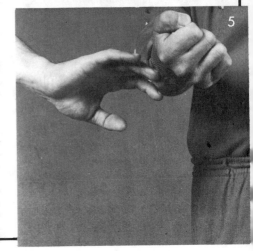

RIGHT WRIST GRAB (ARM DOWN)

The attacker grabs (1) the defender's right wrist while both arms are down. The defender (2-4) turns his arm upward in a counterclockwise direction, applying pressure against the attacker's thumb. The result (5) is that the hold is broken.

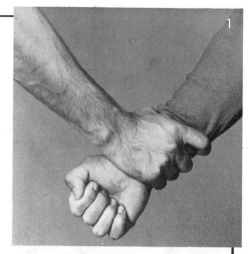

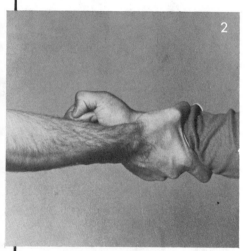

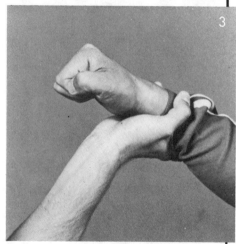

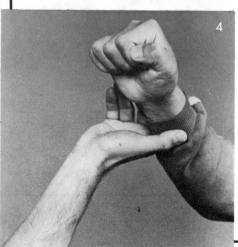

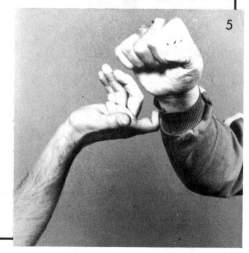

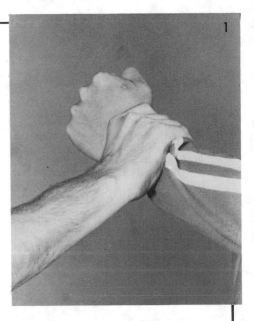

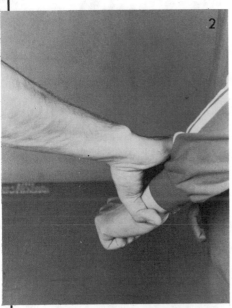

LEFT WRIST GRAB (ARM UP)

The attacker grabs (1) the defender's left wrist while both arms are up. The defender (2-3) turns his arm downward in a clockwise direction, applying pressure against the attacker's thumb. The result (4) is that the hold is broken.

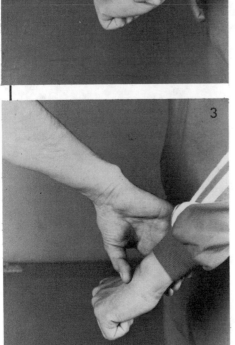

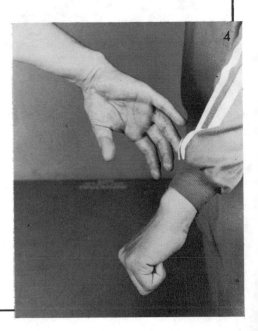

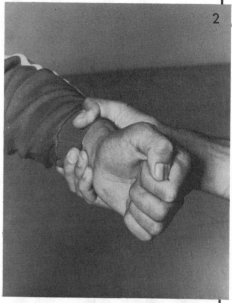

LEFT WRIST GRAB (ARM DOWN)

The attacker grabs (1) the defender's left wrist while both arms are down. The defender (2&3) turns his arm upward in a counterclockwise direction, applying pressure against the attacker's thumb. The result (4) is that the hold is broken.

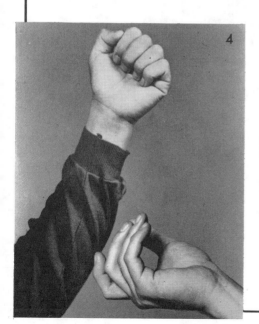

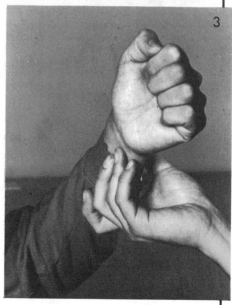

Chapter IV

QUICK-RELEASE VARIATIONS

This chapter contains 13 variations of the quick-release technique. Since the quick release is at the heart of the Chin-Na system, a great deal of attention should be paid to mastering these maneuvers before you move on to the more advanced steps illustrated in part two of this book.

Variation I

QUICK-HAND RELEASE

The attacker (1) grabs the defender's left wrist with his right hand. The defender (2&3) moves his left arm upward, turning his forearm counterclockwise against the attacker's thumb. The result (4) is that the hold is broken. *Note:* This defense

can be used if the defender
is grabbed on the right wrist
by the attacker's left hand.
In that event, the defender's
moves are reversed, in order
to apply the proper pressure
against the attacker's
thumb.

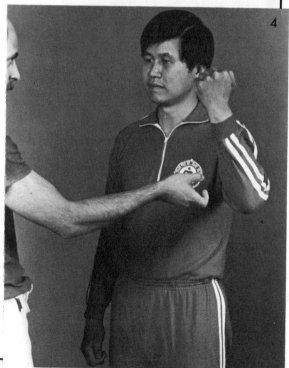

**RIGHT WRIST QUICK
RELEASE (ARM DOWN)**

The attacker (1) grabs the
defender's right wrist with
his right hand. The defender
makes a fist and (2-4)
pushes his arm in a counter-

clockwise circle, applying pressure against the attacker's thumb. The result (5) is that the hold is broken.

Variation III

**RIGHT WRIST QUICK
RELEASE (ARM UP)**

The attacker (1) grabs the defender's right wrist with his right hand while both arms are up. The defender (2-5) rotates his arm clock-

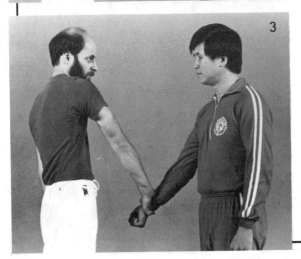

wise and down pushing against the attacker's thumb. The result (6) is that the hold is broken.

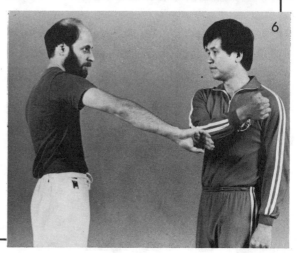

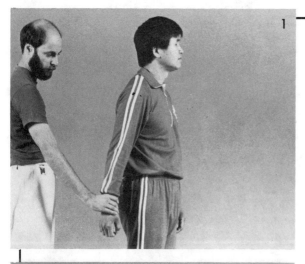

QUICK WRIST RELEASE (FROM BEHIND)

The attacker (1) grabs the defender's right wrist from behind with his right hand. The defender (2) turns toward the attacker, makes a fist and (3-5) completes a

circle in a counterclockwise direction with his arm straight, applying pressure against the attacker's thumb. The result (6) is that the hold is broken.

TWO HAND QUICK RELEASE (ARMS UP)

The attacker (1) grabs the defender's wrists while the defender's arms are raised. The defender (2-4) rotates his right arm counterclockwise and down and his left

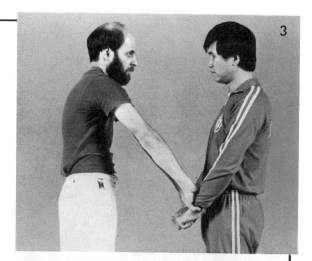

arm clockwise and down across his body, pushing against the attacker's thumbs. The result (5) is that the hold is broken.

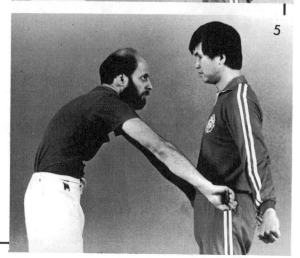

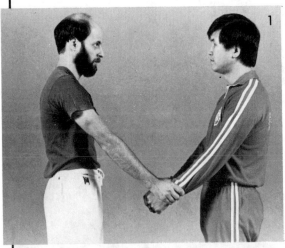

Variation VI

TWO HAND QUICK RELEASE (ARMS DOWN)

The attacker (1) grabs the defender by both wrists. The defender (2&3) rotates his left arm in a clockwise circle and his right arm in a counterclockwise circle,

pushing against both thumbs of the attacker. Simultaneously, he pulls up and bends his elbows during the rotation. The result (4) is that the hold is broken.

Variation VII

TWO HAND QUICK RELEASE (FROM BEHIND)

The attacker (1) grabs both of the defender's wrists from behind. The defender (2) twists clockwise (to the right) to get space between himself and his attacker. Then (3) with his arms extended behind his back, he moves his right arm in a counterclockwise circle, applying pressure against the attacker's right thumb to

break the hold. Finally (4) the defender repeats the technique on the reverse side. His left arm should be fully extended behind his back as he moves it in a clockwise circle, applying pressure against the attacker's left thumb. The result (5) is that the hold is broken.

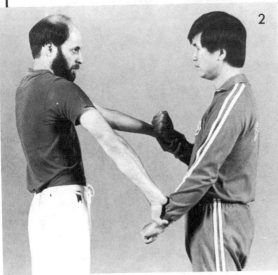

Variation VIII

TWO HAND QUICK RELEASE (VARIATION)

The attacker (1) grabs the defender's left wrist with his right hand (thumb down) and the defender's right wrist with his left hand (thumb up). The defender

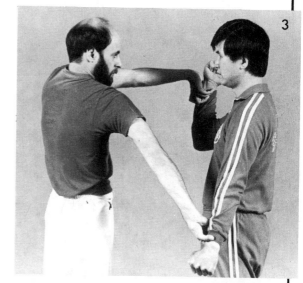

(2&3) rotates both arms clockwise while he pushes against the attacker's thumbs. The result (4) is that the hold is broken.

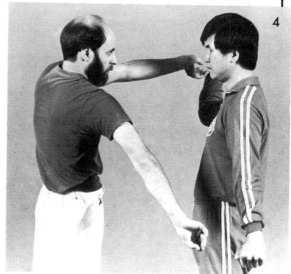

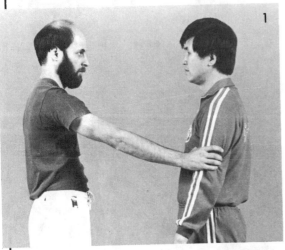

Variation IX

UPPER ARM
QUICK RELEASE

The attacker (1) grabs the defender's left upper arm with his right hand. The defender makes a fist and (2-4) circles his left arm in a counterclockwise circle,

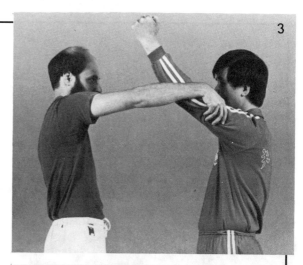

keeping his elbow straight. This motion will press against the attacker's thumb as the top of the circle is completed. The result (5) is that the hold is broken.

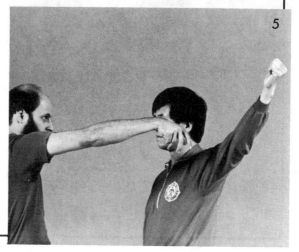

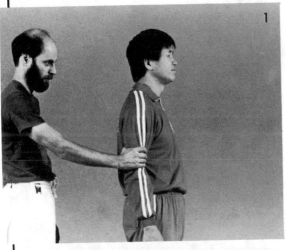

**SINGLE UPPER
ARM QUICK RELEASE
(FROM BEHIND)**

The attacker (1) grabs the defender's right upper arm from behind with his right hand. The defender makes a fist and with his arm straight (2&3) completes a

circle in a counterclockwise direction, applying pressure against the attacker's thumb. The result (4) is that the hold is broken.

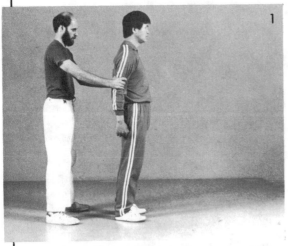

Variation XI

DOUBLE UPPERARM
QUICK RELEASE
(FROM BEHIND)

The attacker (1) grabs both of the defender's upper arms from behind just above the elbow. The defender (2&3) twists clockwise and steps forward with his left foot, bringing his left arm up sharply against the attacker's left wrist. The result (4) is that the de-

fender is able to walk away.
Note: The psychology implicit in this release lies in the feint of looking to the right (in the twist) while the true defense comes from the left when the defender's left arm pushes up abruptly against the attacker's left wrist.

97

Variation XII

CHOKE HOLD QUICK RELEASE

The attacker (1) grabs the defender's neck in a two hand choke hold. The defender (2&3) twists his body to the left and (4) steps back with his left foot as he continues to turn left. The result is that the defender (5) is able to walk away.

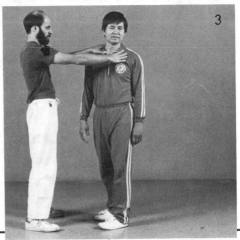

Variation XIII

CHOKE HOLD QUICK RELEASE (FROM BEHIND)

The attacker (1) grabs the defender from behind with a choke hold. The defender (2) turns his body to the left, pushing back against the attacker's right thumb. The result is that the defender (3) is able to walk away.

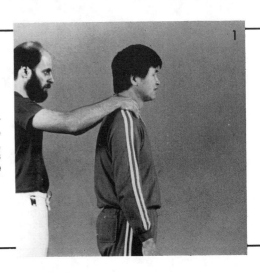

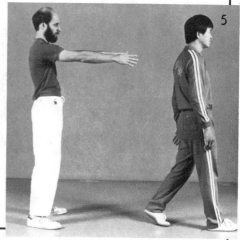

THE EXTENDED TECHNIQUES

As you have seen, the intention of the quick release is to break the hold of your attacker and get away. There will be occasions, however, when you may feel a need to control your attacker more fully. In this situation, the quick release may not be enough of a defense. Such instances require the use of an extended Chin-Na technique.

These techniques are called extended techniques because they require the defender to trap, or otherwise neutralize, the attacker's initial grab before going on to apply the appropriate Chin-Na to control his opponent. This part of the book details examples of T'ien Shan P'ai's extended Chin-Na techniques for various parts of the body.

PART II
Execution

施 行

Chapter V

THE HAIR GRAB

HAIR GRAB I

The attacker (1) has grabbed the defender by the hair with his right hand. The defender (2) in turn, stops the attacker from pulling downward by grabbing the attacker's right hand with his right hand, holding tightly and then (3) by covering his

own right hand with his left and squeezing tightly. Finally (4&5) the defender steps back with his right foot as he bends the attacker's hand backward, and he applies pressure downward.

HAIR GRAB II

The attacker (1) has grabbed the defender by the hair with his right hand. The defender (2), in turn, covers the attacker's hand with his own right hand, holds it tightly, and then (3) covers his own right hand with his left and squeezes tightly. Then (4) the defender twists slightly to the right (clockwise) as he applies pressure downward against the attacker's wrist joint. The result (5) is that the defender controls the attacker to the floor. (A) shows the correct hand grip used in this technique.

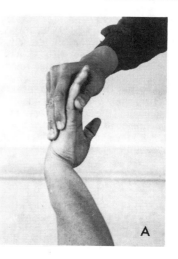

HAIR GRAB III

The attacker (1) has grabbed the defender by the hair from behind with his right hand. The defender (2), in turn, covers the attacker's hand with his right hands, squeezes tightly, and then (3) covers his own right hand with his left hand, and squeezes tightly. What he has done is, he has pinned the attacker's hand against his (the defender's) head. Next (4&5), the defender turns toward the little finger of the attacker's hand. If the attack is made with the right hand, the defender will turn clockwise, and if the attack was made from the left, the defender will turn counterclockwise. Simultaneously, the defender circles under the attacker's outstretched arm, thereby causing the attacker's wrist to bend backwards. Finally (6) the defender applies pressure by pushing upward in a straight line against the attacker's outstretched arm, which (7) brings him under control.

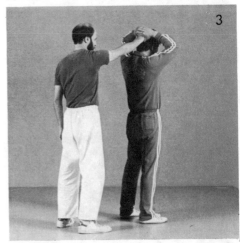

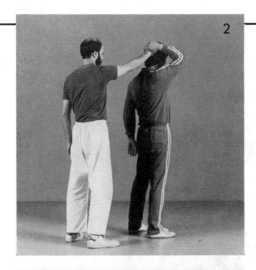

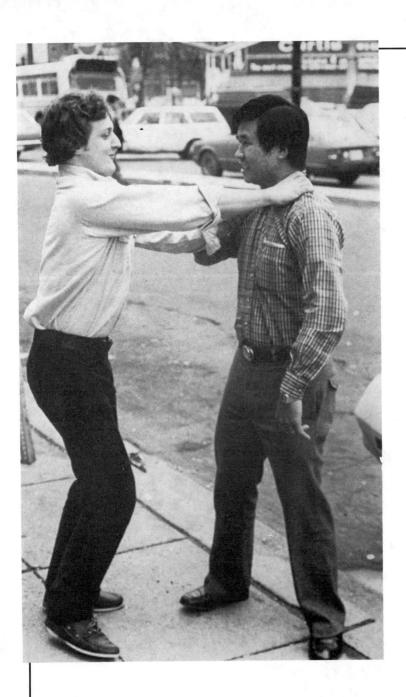

Chapter VI

THE NECK GRAB

NECK GRAB I

The attacker (1) has grabbed the defender's neck with both hands. The defender (2&3) in turn, stretches his arms out, palms up, and raises them outward until they meet over his head. The defender (4) then brings both arms down toward his

stomach and (5) applies pressure against the attacker's elbows, forcing them to bend. With the attacker's arms pinned between the defender's arms and chest, (6) the attacker is completely under control.

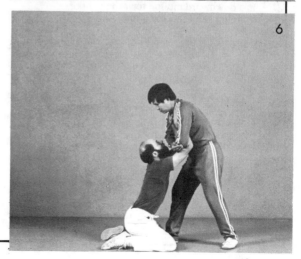

NECK GRAB II

The attacker (1) has grabbed the defender by the neck with both hands. The defender (2&3) in turn moves his left hand between the attacker's arms and traps the attacker's left hand against the defender's right shoulder with the defender's left hand. The defender (4) then moves his right hand in a counterclockwise circle, coming up over the top of the attacker's trapped left hand. Next (5&6) the defender bends his right elbow so that the defender's elbow lines up with the inside crease (the front) of his attacker's elbow, and applies pressure to bend the elbow. Finally (7&8) the defender steps back with his left foot and applies pressure to the attacker's elbow in a downward motion toward the floor, bringing the attacker under control.

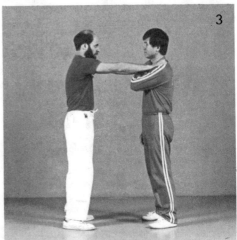

NECK GRAB III

The attacker (1) has grabbed the defender by the neck with both hands. The defender (2&3) in turn brings his hands up inside the attacker's arms and (4&5) twists his body to the left, forces the attacker's left elbow to bend, traps the attacker's left hand under the defender's armpit, and (6&7) brings the attacker under control.

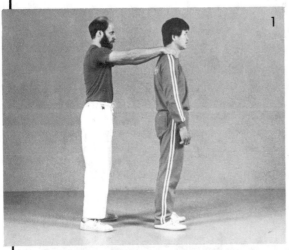

NECK GRAB IV

The attacker (1) has grabbed the defender by the neck from behind with both hands. The defender (2) in turn twists to the right and looks at his opponent. Then (3) he moves his right arm up and over the top of the attacker's left arm. This traps

the attacker's left wrist between the defender's neck and his right shoulder. Finally, keeping the attacker's elbow straight, (4) the defender applies pressure downward and (5) controls the attacker.

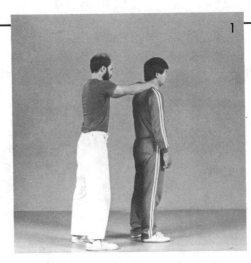

NECK GRAB V

The attacker (1) has grabbed the defender by the neck with both hands from behind. The defender (2), in turn, twists to the right, looking at the attacker. He then (3) steps back with his right foot, and (4-6) moves his right arm up over the attacker's arms, which helps him pin the attacker's arms under his armpits. Finally (7) the defender pulls up on the back of the attacker's elbows and (8) brings him under control.

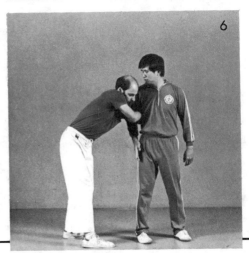

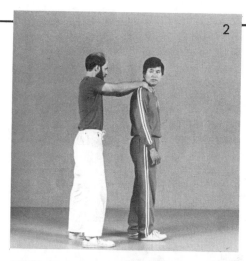

Chapter VII

THE CHEST GRAB

CHEST GRAB I

The attacker has grabbed the defender's shirt front with his right hand. The defender (2), in turn, grabs the attacker's hand with his left hand, trapping it between his hand and chest. The defender (3) then brings his right arm up and over the attacker's arm and hits him on the elbow joint. At the point of impact (4) the defender cracks his wrist in a twisting motion away from his body. The impact (5) forces the attacker's elbow to bend. Finally (6-8) the defender steps back with his left foot (throwing the attacker off balance), pulls back and down on the attacker's elbow joint, and brings him under control.

CHEST GRAB II

The attacker (1) has grabbed the defender by the shirt front with his left hand. The defender (2), in turn, catches the attacker's hand with his left hand, trapping it between his hand and his chest, and squeezes it tightly. Then the defender (3&4) moves his right arm up and under the attacker's left arm, and places his right hand, palm down, against the attacker's chest. Next (5) he steps back with his left foot, and locks his right elbow, making his right arm very rigid. Finally (6&7) the defender bends forward, and downward, (applying pressure against the back of the attacker's elbow) and brings him under control.

CHEST GRAB III

The attacker (1) has grabbed the defender's shirt front with his left hand. The defender (2), in turn, grabs the attacker's hand with his left hand, trapping it between his hand and chest. (*Note:* (A) shows the correct grab used to hold the attacker's hand.) The defender (3) then twists his body to the left, which straightens out the at-

tacker's elbow joint. And finally (4) he leans forward (bending over his own right leg) toward the attacker, twisting the attacker's wrist, forcing the attacker's elbow to bend, and applying pressure to the attacker's inside palm edge all at the same time. The result is that (5) the attacker falls to the floor.

Chapter VIII

THE UPPER-ARM GRAB

UPPER-ARM GRAB I

The attacker (1) has grabbed both the defender's upper arms just above the elbow. The defender (2&3), in turn brings both his arms up in between the attacker's arms. Then (4) the defender turns to the left, as his left arm blocks out the attacker's right arm (on the forearm) and his right arm moves in a clockwise circle over the top of the attacker's left arm (at the elbow). The defender (5) has trapped the attacker's left forearm and hand behind the defender's back by applying the defender's right upper arm to the back of the attacker's elbow. Finally (6) the defender bends his right elbow at the joint, applying pressure upward against the attacker's left elbow, and (7) brings the attacker under control.

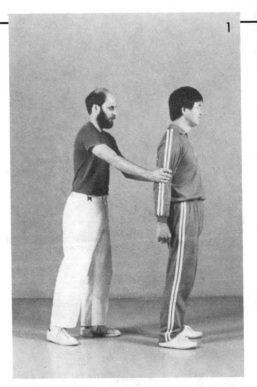

UPPER-ARM GRAB II

The attacker (1) has grabbed both of the defender's upper arms from behind. The defender (2), in reponse turns clockwise, looking at his opponent over his right shoulder. Then (3) the defender steps backward (toward the attacker) with his right foot and (4&5) he moves his right arm in a clockwise circle, blocking the attacker's right hand, and trapping both the attacker's hands under his armpit. Once the attacker's hands are trapped (6) the defender bends his right arm toward his body, applying pressure upward against the backs of the attacker's elbows.

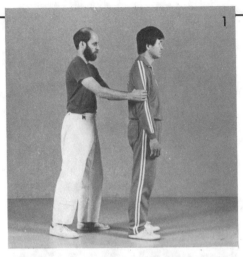

UPPER-ARM GRAB III

The attacker (1) has grabbed both the defender's upper arms from behind. The defender (2), in response, turns clockwise looking at the attacker over his right shoulder. Then (3) the defender steps back with his right foot toward the attacker as his right arm (4) moves in a counterclockwise circle down and under the attacker's left arm, catching his left upper arm just above the elbow. Finally (5-7) the defender applies a rolling pressure downward, bringing the attacker under control.

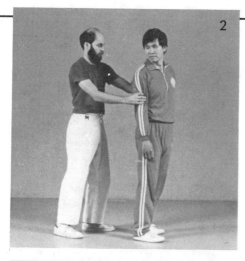

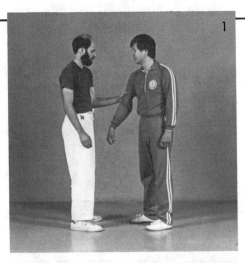

UPPER-ARM GRAB IV

The attacker (1) has grabbed the defender's upper right arm. In response (2) the defender traps the attacker's left hand with his left hand. (The attacker's hand becomes pinned between the defender's hand and upper arm.) He then raises his right arm (3-5) moving it in a counterclockwise circle until his elbow rests on the attacker's wrist joint. Next (6) he applies pressure to the attacker's wrist joint, forcing the attacker's elbow to bend outward. Finally (7) the defender steps backward with his left foot, pulling the attacker down and backward by his wrist joint. The line of pull should be straight down to the defender's left toe.

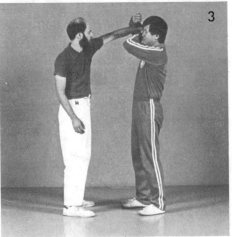

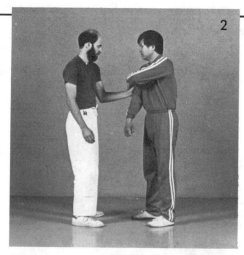

Chapter IX

THE FOREARM GRAB

FOREARM GRAB I

The defender (1) stands with his arms folded across his chest (right arm on top) as the attacker approaches. The attacker (2) pushes the defender with both hands against the defender's right forearm. The defender (3) stops the push with his right forearm, and moves his left arm backward toward his own body. Then (4) the defender's left hand comes around to trap the attacker's right hand (his left palm should completely cover the back of the attacker's right hand). Finally (5), the defender pushes down on the attacker's wrist joint with his left hand and turns his own right hand in a circular motion (away from his body) so that the attacker's hand is pinned between the defender's two hands. The defender twists the attacker's hand clockwise and backward, all the while applying pressure down and toward the attacker's center, which (6&7) puts the attacker under control.

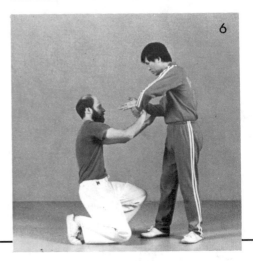

FOREARM GRAB II

The defender (1) stands with his arms folded across his chest (right arm on top) as the attacker approaches. The attacker (2) pushes the defender with both hands against the defender's right forearm. The defender stops the push (3) with his right forearm and moves his hand between the attacker's arms (from below) to trap the attacker's left hand. (The defender's left palm should completely cover the back of the attacker's left hand.) The edge of the defender's hand should be parallel with the attacker's wrist joint. Finally (4), the defender presses the attacker's Tiger Mouth (see page 68) with his left hand and moves his right elbow in a circular motion (away from his body). He is pushing against the attacker's inside palm edge, twisting the attacker's hand counterclockwise and backwards, all the while applying pressure down and toward the attacker's center. The result is (5&6) that the defender controls the attacker as the defender pushes him toward the floor.

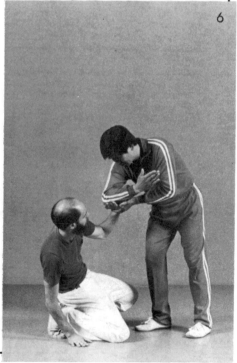

FOREARM GRAB III

The defender (1) stands with his arms folded across his chest (right arm on top) as the attacker approaches. The attacker (2) pushes the defender with both arms. In response, (3) the defender turns his body to the left, letting the attacker's left hand land on the outside of the defender's right shoulder. At the same time, he traps the attacker's left hand against the back of his shoulder by using his own left hand. Next (4), he rotates his shoulder in a circular motion away from his own body, pushing against the attacker's inside palm edge, which twists the attacker's hand counterclockwise and backwards. He should also apply pressure downward and toward the attacker's center. Finally (5) the defender controls the attacker by pushing him toward the floor.

146

2

4

5

Chapter X

THE WRIST GRAB

WRIST GRAB I

The attacker (1) has grabbed the defender's right wrist with his left hand. In response (2&3) the defender moves his left hand in a circular (clockwise) motion and grabs the attacker's wrist (which should trap it between the defender's hand and wrist), and at the same time he should "slip" his hand upward and behind the attacker's wrist. (*Note:* (A) shows the correct wrist grab; (B) shows the defender's "slip" motion). Next (4) the defender moves his right arm in a counterclockwise circle until his hand is in front of the center of his own body. His elbow should be bent, and he should force the attacker's elbow to straighten during the circular move. As the defender (5) continues to rotate his right wrist counterclockwise, he will catch the attacker's wrist joint from underneath, which he should push down on while pulling up with his fingers on the attacker's forearm. Then (6) he should apply a twist to bend the attacker's elbow, making sure he keeps his own elbow straight. Finally (7) the defender applies pressure downward and toward the attacker's center, forcing the attacker to the floor. When that is completed (8) the defender can push the attacker away.

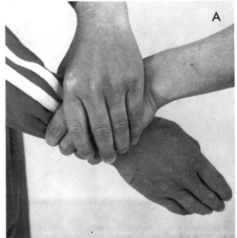

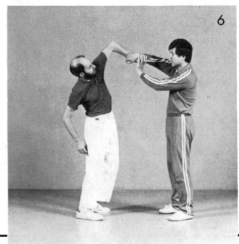

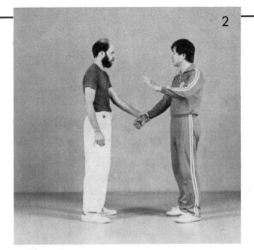

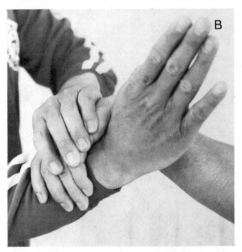

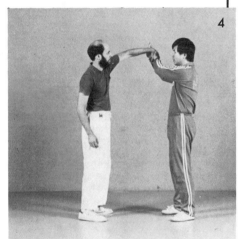

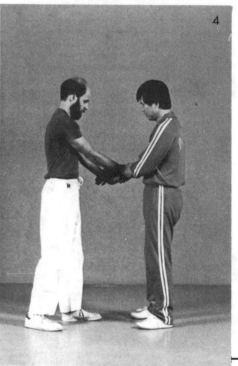

WRIST GRAB II

The attacker (1) has grabbed both the defender's wrists. In response (2) the defender moves his left hand counterclockwise to trap the attacker's left hand from underneath. He should grab the attacker's hand tightly. Then (3&4) the defender rotates his right hand sharply to the right so that his fingers point to the ceiling. (His right wrist will still be encircled by the attacker's left hand grip during the rotation.) The result (5&6) is that the defender controls the attacker.

WRIST GRAB III

The attacker (1) has grabbed both the defender's wrists. In response (2) the defender pulls his hands in toward the center, waist level, throwing the attacker off balance. Then (3) the defender traps the attacker's left wrist with his left hand, trapping it between his hand and wrist. (This movement will also act as a release on the attacker's right hand grab.) Next (4), the defender moves his right arm in a counterclockwise circle until his hand is in front of the center of his own body. His elbow should be bent, and he should force the attacker's elbow to straighten during the circular move. As the defender continues to rotate his right wrist counterclockwise, (5&6) he should catch the attacker's wrist joint from underneath, pushing down with his fingers on the attacker's forearm and apply a twist so that the attacker's elbow bends. At the end of this movement, the defender's elbow should be straight. Finally (7) the defender applies pressure down and toward the attacker's center with his right hand fingers. This will force the attacker to the floor. After that is completed, (8) the defender may push the attacker away.

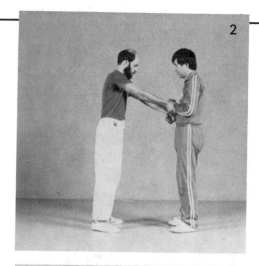

WRIST GRAB IV

The attacker (1) has grabbed both of the defender's wrists from behind. In response (2) the defender twists to the right, looking at his attacker. He then (3&4) moves his right hand in a clockwise circle, guiding the attacker's left hand in a counterclockwise direction as he comes over the top of the attacker's left arm. (With this movement, the defender pins the attacker's hands and forearms between the defender's right elbow and the right side of his body.) Next (5) he applies pressure with his right forearm against the back of the attacker's left elbow and (6) brings the attacker under control.

WRIST GRAB V

The attacker (1) has grabbed both of the defender's wrists from behind. In response (2) the defender twists to the right, looking at the attacker. He then (3&4) moves his right arm in a counterclockwise circle under the attacker's left arm. Finally (5) he applies pressure to the back of the attacker's left elbow and (6) brings him under control.

158

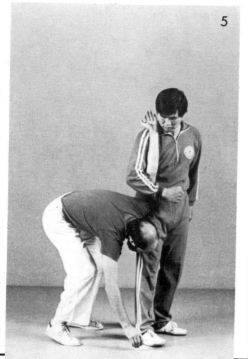